A Touch of C

by
Judy Condon

Library of Congress Cataloging-in-Publications Data
A Touch of Country by Judy Condon
ISBN 978-0-9843332-8-8

Oceanic Graphic Printing, Inc.
105 Main Street
Hackensack, NJ 07601

Printed in China

Layout and Design by Pat Lucas
Edited by Trent Michaels

Table of Contents

Introduction 5

Chapter 1 6
Alice and Michael Lezu

Chapter 2 23
Leslie and Steven Powell

Chapter 3 44
Charlotte and Tom Whitlatch

Chapter 4 59
Linda and Don Kuzak

Chapter 5 72
Sharyn and Lloyd Sheats

Chapter 6 88
Candace and Bob Littiken

Chapter 7 102
Ed Oestreich

Chapter 8 129
Betty Jean and Jack Dalrymple

About the Author

Judy Condon is a native New Englander, which is evident in her decorating style and the type of antiques she collects and sells. Her real passion is 19thC authentic dry red or blue painted pieces. While Judy enjoyed a professional career as a teacher, Principal and Superintendent of Schools in Connecticut, Judy's weekends were spent at her antique shop, *Marsh Homestead Country Antiques*, located in Litchfield, Connecticut.

When her husband, Jeff, was relocated to Virginia, Judy accepted an early retirement from education and concentrated her energy and passion for antiques into a fulltime business. Judy maintains a website, *www.marshhomesteadantiques.com* and has been a Power Seller on ebay® for over thirteen years under the name "superct".

Judy and her husband Jeff recently returned to their roots in New England and have just completed renovating a 19thC home in Massachusetts which will be featured in the next book, *Back Home*. Judy has five children and five grandchildren and enjoys reading, golf, Bridge, tennis and volunteering in the educational system in St Maarten. Judy has been in the process of providing teaching materials and children's books to the schools in St. Maarten with the hopes of helping to establish classroom libraries.

Judy's first seventeen books in the "simply country" series, *Country on a Shoestring, Of Hearth and Home – Simply Country, A Simpler Time, Country Decorating for All Seasons, As Time Goes By, Country at Heart, Welcome Home – Simply Country, Home Again – Simply Country, The Warmth of Home, The Country Home, Simple Greens – Simply Country , The Country Life, Simply Country Gardens, The Spirit of Country, The Joy of Country* and *Holidays at a Country Home* have been instant hits and most are already in their second printing. Judy may be reached through her website *www.marshhomesteadantiques.com*, her email address, *marshhomestead@comcast.ne*t or by phone at 877-381-6682.

Introduction
to
A Touch of Country

Someone recently said to me, "Country decorating isn't a style; it's a way a life". I've found as I've traveled and visited hundreds of country decorated homes, that even though "country" encompasses a wide variety of styles, a common thread binds us. We love to nestle in our homes and never tire of adding or replacing a piece. Some of us putter, some of us tinker, but we are all entertained by our homes; they amuse and occupy us. It is part of our life to tirelessly hunt for new treasures and create a home for our new find.

However, I find myself asking, "Is there such a thing as a 'touch' of country?" Many of you, as I do, try to downsize and simplify, if for no other reason than to offer the sense that we are making our hectic lives more manageable. But I must confess that when Jeff and I downsized from a 3,700 square foot home to one measuring slightly more than 1,600, my goal was to fit every one of my cherished pieces into our new home! Not only did I do it, I even added a few. For that reason, I ponder whether or not just a touch of country is really possible, as I'm often forced to restrain myself with my collecting and decorating. Most recently, Jane and Barron Hansen, whom I met when I filmed their nearby home for the last holiday book, offered to help age my walls. I forced myself to confine our artistic talents to the Keeping Room and hold at bay the impulse to cover every plastered wall with antiquing glaze. I plan to include the before and after pictures of our 1825 remodeled Cape in my next book entitled *Back Home*.

In this book, you will tour the homes of the Powell family in Connecticut, Ed Oestreich of Maine, the Sheats family of Delaware, the Lezu family in New Hampshire, the Littikens of Indiana, and lastly the Whitlatch and Kuzak families in Ohio. Note how each family has "just" *A Touch of Country*!

Chapter 1

Alice and Michael Lezu

Alice and Michael's gardens were featured earlier this year in *Simply Country Gardens*, in which I mentioned that the Lezus love to move– and in fact, their home is for sale at the time of this writing. They are ready once more to pack up, having found a home in North Carolina. Michael and Alice have lived in New Hampshire for 15 years and purchased this reproduction colonial in Claremont from renowned Early American floor cloth artist Dennis Belanger and his wife Sheila. The Lezus would like to be closer to their two grown sons, both of whom live in the south. Michael's position as a manager with K-Mart allows the Lezus to move often.

The outside of the house is painted with Olde Century "Thistle" paint. The scroll above the door was one of the few changes Michael and Alice made to the house.

I have never been in a home featuring a wider variety of collections. I complimented Alice often as I filmed, as her home is like a beautiful country shop. The formal living room is on the left side of the front of the house. Dennis Belanger painted the colorful canvas floor cloth. The blue cupboard in the corner is a reproduction purchased at The Seraph in Sturbridge, Massachusetts. The trim color of the room is a Seraph color called "Prushian Blue". The drop leaf maple table dates to the early 1800's and was found in Vermont.

Michael and Alice both like the artwork of Kolene Spicher and keep many of her prints throughout their home, including the whale hanging above the trencher filled with fruit.

Michael and Alice found the portrait hanging above the mantel at an auction in Massachusetts. Alice purchased the small hooked rug at a local country shop. The small watercolor was a gift from a friend; it stands on the table beside an early flask.

A built-in bookcase holds a collection of leather-bound books, an early decanter on the top shelf, and a ceramic bust of George Washington.

The top portrait in the picture on the top right depicts the son of Franklin Pierce, the 14th President of the United States and only president to hail from New Hampshire. A basket holds raw flax on top of the corner cupboard.

A grain painted dome-lidded box made by folk artist Helen Howard rests atop an early secretary desk. Michael's appreciation of watercolors comes from his childhood; he selected the Spicher print above the desk.

The William and Mary chest is a first period replica. The portrait was found in Massachusetts. The sewing basket on the ladderback chair was one of the first antiques Alice's parents, former antique dealers, gave her.

The walls in the front hall were stenciled by Dennis Belanger, who also made the floor cloth.

The chest dates to the late 1700's and was found in Vermont. Kathy Graybill painted the tavern sign above it. The matching wall sconces were found at a craft show.

Alice owns over 85 redware pieces. Many of the pieces displayed on the black cupboard in the dining room were done by Gregg Schooner or David T. Smith. The trim paint is Olde Century "Olde Pewter".

Redware Christmas balls, gourds, and a tin pineapple found at a garage sale fill the trencher. All of the pewter pieces, with the exception of the plates, are early.

The table is a single board farm table found in Vermont.

In this room, Alice prefers the openness of windows without treatments.

The small Windsor chair was purchased in Eden, New York, at the Kazoo factory. The "man in the moon" doll was purchased at a folk art shop in Vermont. The stoneware jugs beneath the sideboard are all A.P. Donaghho and were part of Alice's late father's collection.

Alice's counter and farm sink are Vermont soapstone, which she loves. She reported that she has oiled the counter to just the perfect color. Alice uses two paints in her kitchen, Sherwin Williams colors from their historic Mt. Vernon paint collection–"Iron Chest" and "Tobacco Leaf".

A reproduction lantern known as a Whaler's Lantern hangs over the island. The bottom bowl is an early burl bowl.

Built-in bookcases provide an ideal display area for more of Alice's redware. Alice painted the board beneath the "Hands to Work" sign above the microwave.

The rooster sitting on the wooden block is actually a birdhouse!

Alice's kitchen opens up to a large eating area and family room spanning the back of the house. The sliding glass door opens to a screened porch off the back of the house. The table in the center of the room is a tilt-top. Dennis Belanger painted the mustard and bittersweet colored floor cloth.

Alice displays her Santa collection in the large mustard Vermont cupboard dating to the mid 1800's.

The Santa figures on the right side of the bottom row were made by Michael and Alice's two sons.

The blue cupboard in the back corner is early but the doors are newly painted with Rufus Porter type scenes. The tavern table in front of the couch is late 1700's. The top was badly burned from a candle so Alice and Michael flipped the top over.

The three-legged table in the back is an early piece found in Vermont.

The reproduction horse weathervane provides a great silhouette against the window.

The portrait over the mantel was found on Cape Cod. The coverlet is mid-19thC and drapes over a wing armchair which Alice bought for $25 at a flea market; she loved the mouse hole in the back.

The single bed in the guestroom is rope-tied. The rug is from The Seraph.

Alice displays some of her folk art doll collection in this guestroom.

The chest of drawers in the corner is early, while the horse pull toy is a reproduction.

The hooked rug over the bed was found at a local country shop.

The model ship on the hanging shelf in a second guestroom belonged to Michael's grandfather. Alice's father had her mother's initials and date of her passing added to the crazy quilt draped on the back of the chair.

Another Spicher print hangs between the windows in the second guestroom. The tin butcher-chasing-the-pig folk art piece on the shelf is a reproduction.

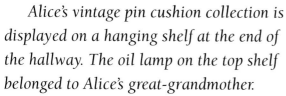

Alice's vintage pin cushion collection is displayed on a hanging shelf at the end of the hallway. The oil lamp on the top shelf belonged to Alice's great-grandmother.

The eagle tavern sign over the bed in the third guestroom was painted by Kathy Graybill. The black and linen coverlet and shams are from Family Heirloom Weavers of Pennsylvania.

A trunk filled with Santa figures is displayed year round.

Alice used a wire tree to display her old and new Christmas ornaments.

Alice used "Prushian Blue" paint from The Seraph for the trim in this guestroom.

I liked the look of the stenciled floor in the master bedroom, but Alice said she was anxious to sand it and oil the plain pine boards. The cupboard in the back features a new base and old top with pastoral scenes painted on the doors.

Two early canvas landscapes hang above a small candlestand at one end of the room.

Dennis Belanger made the fireplace board. The bed warmer belonged to Alice's mother's family, as did the chamber pot.

I joked with Alice about her next move and told her, "You have so many things; you could open your doors and have a sale like a shop when you move." I learned that is exactly what she plans to do sometime in the fall. By the time this book goes to print, the house may already have been sold and the antique sale completed-but if interested, please contact Alice via her email, alicelezu@gmail.com.

Chapter 2

Leslie and Steven Powell

Leslie Powell and I first met 15 years ago when our daughters became friends in high school. I recall Leslie's husband Steven picking up his daughter and going home to tell Leslie perhaps she should call me as it appeared from our homes that we shared a common interest in country antiques. From that point we became friends and soon made Thursday afternoons our weekly golf outing and early Saturday mornings our flea market adventure. Leslie is one of those collectors who had the foresight years ago to collect and relish the beauty of painted pieces long before they were popular and at a time when so many of us were stripping or dipping our paint away! As a result, Leslie's collection is extensive and beautifully displayed in their 1777 home built in Bantam, Connecticut, by Jonathan Page. Despite the fact that Steven is well over 6' tall and the ceilings are not, (I presented him with a hard hat as a housewarming gift!), they purchased the house and began to renovate to accommodate a few minor details, such as the fact that their bedroom furniture would not fit up the stairs! Leslie's dream had always been to operate an antique shop, and the property included a building formerly used as a shop. Her dream came true 13 years ago.

Within a year, an addition off the back of the house had been remodeled into a master bedroom and a master carpenter called in to recreate the kitchen. Steven and Leslie chose Kyanize "Colonial Red" for the house and outbuildings and Old Village "Antique Pewter" for the trim, while also stenciling the dining room floor. The patio was built with stones gathered from the property.

Water trickles from a pond at the back of the house through a small brook between the house and Leslie's shop, Toll House Antiques.

Three years of growth of thyme, planted between patio stones, provides a colorful carpet. The bonus is that the more the thyme is walked on, the faster it spreads.

Leslie's shop, shown above, is further described at the end of the chapter.

A side porch is filled with comfortable wicker and overlooks the brook and country gardens behind the garage.

Leslie has placed exquisite pieces in every nook and cranny. In the laundry room, a 19thC hanging cupboard in red wash holds early fabric covered books and a Schneeman sewing box. The vintage jar on top holds a collection of bake-o-lite buttons.

A beautiful blue painted early basket hangs on a peg above an apothecary jar with tin lid filled with early wooden knitting needles.

A collection of Rockingham clay marbles are displayed in a jar on top of the 19thC oxblood red table found at The Elephant Trunk. Leslie was ecstatic to find the small shelf above for $10, which she uses to display her small and diminutive baskets.

Leslie and Steven purchased their couch at Angle House in West Brookfield, Massachusetts. The oil on canvas portrait was found at a large flea market periodically held in Stormville, New York. Leslie shops weekly at The Elephant Trunk, a flea market in New Milford, Connecticut, where she has found numerous pieces over the years. The corner cupboard in early pewter paint was being unloaded from the vendor's Jeep when Leslie purchased it for $60.

One of Leslie's favorite paints is "Valley Forge Mustard" by Old Village. She admits, though, that the color improves as it ages. Leslie learned that two tablespoons of talcum powder per gallon will eliminate the shine of new paint. The large round table with oxblood red paint was another Elephant Trunk find. The doughbowl is an old bowl with newly applied paint.

A collection of 19thC samplers hangs to the right of the mantel.

Leslie purchased the early lidded box at a local tag sale. A small berry basket sits on top. Six hogscrapers with douters line the mantel on the right side. The jug and bottle on the left are early.

Leslie purchased the child's chair from Mary Elliott of Massachusetts. A 19thC lollipop candlebox with wonderful patina hangs above.

The large 19thC hanging pewter shelf features lovely dry salmon paint and provides the ideal spot to display early pewter. The six-board chest in red wash below it holds four early stoneware jugs.

Helen Howard of Connecticut created the mustard diamond patterned floor cloth in the sitting room.

A 19thC stretcher base tavern table holds a beautiful early blue trencher. Leslie has filled it with faux pale gold apples providing a nice contrast to the blue and tying in with the floor cloth.

Leslie couldn't resist the hanging wall shelf in original attic surface; the sawtooth cutout at the base made it a "have to have". The collection of leather bound books blends beautifully with the tones of the original shelf.

Sunlight streaming in from the bay window creates a silhouette of the early rocking horse in mustard paint, which sits on a large, two-board top farm table at the side of the room.

The red, feather-painted chest is Leslie's favorite of the stack seen in the corner.

The oil on canvas above the camelback sofa was purchased at a Weston Thorne auction in Litchfield, Connecticut. Note the beautiful wear of the blue paint on the gathering basket. Four New England jugs stand beneath the bench which serves as a coffee table.

The trim in this room is done with Old Village "Rittenhouse Green".

Two early wooden puppet heads are seen in the lower right corner of the built-in bookcase.

An alcove off the sitting rooms is filled with early bowls, firkins, baskets, and buckets in paint.

This area was difficult to photograph because of its size; obviously Leslie utilizes every available inch for display.

A fan of old paint could linger in this room for hours without tiring of the beauty of the various surfaces!

Steven and Leslie converted the addition on the back of the house to include the master bedroom, not only because none of their furniture could fit up the stairs, but Steven at 6' 5" was forced to crouch while walking anywhere upstairs in the original section.

The early child's rocking horse was a recent acquisition and blends beautifully with the muted blue and white tones of the room.

The basket on the chest of drawers conceals a telephone.

The fireplace in the kitchen is what convinced Leslie to purchase the house. She chose Old Village "Salem Brick Red" in the kitchen.

Some of Leslie's butter press collection is seen on the mantel. The cupboard above is filled with early stoneware.

More of Leslie's painted bowls are tucked in the corner on the rack and atop a single board 19thC jelly cupboard in blue.

Leslie's counters are constructed of wide pine boards.
An early stoneware cake crock sits in the middle of the early red base scrub top pine table.

Leslie used "Antique Pewter" Old Village paint in the dining room. The Hitchcock chairs were purchased from the home's previous owners.

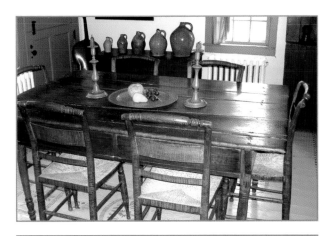

Leslie and a friend stenciled the floor in this room using "Antique Pewter" and "Salem Brick Red" Old Village paint. The large stepback was purchased at Brimfield during our first trip there years ago. Leslie worried the entire trip home about how much it had cost, yet today could sell it for two to three times what she paid. It is filled with early pewter pieces, many of which were purchased at a local flea market.

An early bench holds more buckets and firkins in paint. Two early chairs hang from a peg rack, while a portion of the stenciled floor is visible in the corner.

The cello dates to the late 1700's; it stands beside a 19thC six-board chest in red and beneath a 19thC unsigned American oil on canvas of mother and child.

Brown manganese jugs and crocks, some Schooner, fill the small hanging red 19thC cupboard.

Two birdcage Windsor chairs stand on either side of a small pine scrub top table. More of the intricately stenciled floor is visible.

Large pewter chargers line the mantel of one of the home's three working fireplaces.

Leslie used Old Village "British Red" in the guestroom upstairs.

A crock filled with tin red flowers stands on a small Sheraton table in the corner.

The bonnet, found at Brimfield, is early and rests on top of a 19thC cottage pine bureau alongside pieces made by Jennifer Schneeman.

Leslie made the sampler above the bed.
The doll seen left is early and features a
redware head.

A 19thC rope bed in red is covered with an early coverlet. In the corner, a cheese safe with original salmon paint holds a stack of vintage textiles.

The peg rack is built into the wall and original to the house.

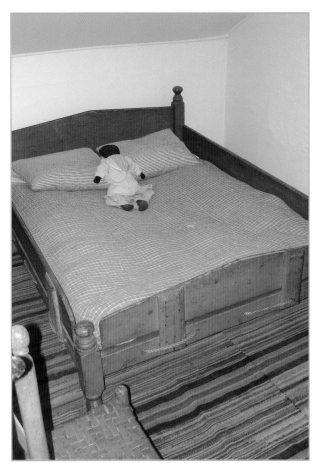

A picker stopped by Leslie's shop and offered the blue rope bed for next to nothing. The hanging red open shelf holds a collection of stuffed animals by Barbara Stein.

Leslie's shop, Toll House Antiques, is open by appointment.

Leslie specializes in early country, candles, stoneware, painted pieces, and accessories.
She may be reached at 860-567-3130 or by email: tollhouseantiques@yahoo.com. Her Website is
www.litchfieldct.com/ant/tollhse/tollhse.html.

Chapter 3

Charlotte and Tom Whitlatch

Charlotte, or Char, as she prefers to be called, grew up on a farm 10 miles down the road in Cadiz, Ohio. As a child Char was bedridden with rheumatic fever and refused to eat. Her father promised that if she was good and ate her food, he would buy her a pony. Within days, Char looked out her bedroom window, and there was her pony. That was the beginning of her father's farm where he raised cattle and quarter horses. Tom owns a body shop in town and has collected gas station memorabilia such as old gas pumps, which he reconditions. Tom owns two vintage Corvettes and also drag raced, which is how Char was first introduced to antiques. While at a race, with extra time on her hands, Char walked into a nearby shop operated by the late Jim Booth and his wife, Mary, in Mt. Vernon, Ohio. At that moment Char knew what she liked and wanted to do with her home. Incidentally, Mary Booth's home was featured in *Home Again– Simply Country* in 2009.

Char and Tom's house was built in 1955; they have lived there since 1972.

A friend and her husband made the birdhouse on the front porch.

Upon entering the house, a visitor passes into the "sewing room". A pull toy horse, made with real horse hair, sits atop an apple green-over-red jelly cupboard. The blue painted table was an Ohio find.

Char purchased the red corner cupboard covered with thick black enamel paint. Using a heat gun and knife, Char stripped the enamel and uncovered a dry red wash. A chalky white basket holds clusters of bittersweet on top.

The blue-gray cupboard seen above came from a Wells Fargo depot; it retains the stamp across the top and original paperwork on the inside.

Char and Tom have collected over 85 pieces of stoneware. Char said when they began collecting, they bought a few pieces with cracks, but now only consider mint condition stoneware.

The dry sink was purchased from an Ohio dealer and looks to be a Pennsylvania piece. The hanging blue-green cupboard above holds green and white graniteware. Char also has collected over 400 blue and white spatterware, most of which she stores.

Char recently started rug hooking and utilizes an old store bin to separate and store her wools.

The all-original 9', two-board farm table in the kitchen was a work table in a barn. It was about to be burned when Char and Tom rescued it. A married set of chairs from Char's family surround the table. The pie safe with blue paint in the background retains its original tins.

Tom Metz, a friend from Paoli, Ohio, makes the treenware seen on the table.

Char's kitchen cabinets were red when they moved in and then Tom and Char painted them mustard. Everyone thought they were too dark, so she painted them blue to match the cook stove in the corner. Amish builders created the countertops with wood from an old mill. The farm sink is soapstone.

Char loves apothecaries and displays a
number of them throughout the house. The
apothecary seen above was bought from a friend
who found it in West Virginia.

The hole above the sink was once a window.
When one of Tom's Corvettes stored in the
basement under the kitchen caught fire and
caused extensive damage to the house, Tom and
Char treated it as an opportunity to open the
back wall and add a large room.

The blue and white porcelain gas stove in
the corner proved to be the beginning of Char's
blue and white spatterware collection. She
would like to replace the stove but Tom has
moved it enough times to know he doesn't want
to move it again.

The shutters hide the spot where a window used to be. The red butcher block table holds an apothecary found in Pennsylvania.

Char keeps a piece of homespun over the stove that she uses for everyday cooking, which she admits is minimal because removing all the doughboards is too much of an effort!

Char and Tom finished the upstairs and are ready to stain the pine walls and ceilings. The coverlets are from Family Heirloom Weavers of Pennsylvania.

The blue standing doughbox was purchased from the same dealer who sold Char the gray pie safe in the back corner. The rocking cradle was found in Pennsylvania.

Nieces and nephews enjoy visiting and sleeping in the handyman's bed off the sewing room.

The blanket roll bed in the master bedroom was purchased at a West Virginia auction. The coverlet is from Family Heirloom Weavers. The horse on top of the red jelly cupboard was also found in West Virginia. Tom added doors to the cupboard and friend Sally Whims painted them to match.

Char and Tom use an old doll's bed for their dog.

Tom and friends built the large room across the back of the house. The fireplace is 11' wide. Char placed an old French door on the mantel and has hung Sweet Annie from it.

An early berry carrier holds potted herbs.

The 8' farm table with two-board top comes in handy when the family gets together.

The shelves above the table hold a collection of candleboxes and painted buckets.

Placed to the right of the fireplace, an old West Virginia cupboard on wheels with wonderful patina was once used in a tobacco factory.

The large early jelly cupboard houses computer equipment. Another apothecary sits on top of a bucket bench with a 34" wide single-board end.

The settle is the first settle Sally Whim's made. Beside it, three coverlets are displayed, all from Cadiz, Ohio.

An early bucket bench with yellow paint holds a large crock with a flower salt-glazed cobalt decoration.

A large screen porch overlooks the back yard. The early farm table with red base belonged to Tom's grandmother. A primitive bucket bench with green paint holds stoneware at the far end, while a cobbler's bench serves as a coffee table in front of the twig settle.

A tall chalky white cupboard holds a folk art log house on top – a perfect expression of what is in the backyard!

The log cabin once stood behind a home for the elderly in nearby Harrison County, Ohio. Tom bought the cabin from a logger and hired a truck for two days to move the 1820's cabin, log by log, to the backyard. Tom and friends constructed the frame and the Amish finished the roof and flooring. An old wash tub, wood bin, and original goat cart decorate the front porch.

The inside is charming! The first floor features a Great Room which Char has tastefully divided into separate areas. In the back, an early table with a two-board top creates a dining area.

The large gray cupboard, which Char found at the Booth's shop and got her started collecting, provides more shelf display for stoneware crocks.

The fireplace bricks came from an old brick schoolhouse in a nearby town.

The upstairs also features a single room- filled with twin and double beds and a trundle bed for young guests.

Char is always looking for pieces and enjoys meeting and speaking with fellow collectors.
She willingly offered her email for anyone who might wish to contact her. Char can be reached at
pumpwizard@frontier.com.

Chapter 4

❧ ✿ ❧

Linda and Don Kuzak

Occasionally when I am traveling to a home to photograph, I pass by a house that catches my eye. While driving to Mogador, Ohio, to photograph the home of Don and Linda Kuzak, I had inadvertently added a digit to their street number and admiringly passed their home three times in my effort to find where I was supposed to be. I was thrilled when I discovered that the house I had noticed was indeed Don and Linda's. The minute I pulled into the driveway, I was enthralled with the picket-fenced garden across the front and the whimsical nature of the garden ornaments.

Linda and Don's story is like a novel. Don grew up in Mogador while Linda moved from California as a high school senior. After high school, Don joined the Army and Linda moved away. Five years ago they reconnected, married three years later, and now live six houses away from the high school where they met. Don is a retired art and special education teacher, which partly explains their creative and imaginative home.

Linda lived in Florida for a number of years and was unable to satisfy her passion for gardening there. Linda admits that she "went crazy" when she moved back to Ohio.

Don contributes artistic elements such as "Ina Demby", a whimsical tin and wood figure Don made in memory of a neighbor. As a child he watched Ms Demby throw sticks to free cherries from the tree.

A weathered wooden mushroom is one of two Linda and Don purchased for $5 from a stunned antique dealer who couldn't believe anyone would want them.

An old milk wagon rests beside a primitive sundial.

Don made the whale from wood found in an old mill in Amish country. I immediately commissioned Don to make one for me!

The large front porch is beautifully shaded with mature trees providing a tranquil setting. The hanging swing dates to the early 20thC. Sweet Annie hangs from a peg rack over a cupboard Linda found in Florida.

Stepping through the front door gives a visitor a sense of traveling through time. Don and Linda discovered a large quantity of old fencing in a dumpster at the transfer station. They took it all and, using drywall compound to fill the gaps, created a log cabin effect throughout the first floor of their home. The shutters conceal a bay window and a television on the sill. The hanging candleholder was made by Joyce Hershman, owner of the nearby Seville Antique Center. Linda purchased the George Washington print at a thrift shop in Florida.

The desk shown left is a perfect example of how antiques travel. The desk was sold by Marjorie Staufer, featured in The Country Life, to Chris Cefus, featured in Welcome Home. And now Don and Linda have purchased the piece from Chris.

The lift-top blanket chest dates to the late 1700's and was found in Medina, Ohio; it retains its original tear drop pulls and original surface. Two old leather German Bibles rest on top.

The blue-green corner cupboard is an early piece purchased from the owner of a B&B in Florida. Remnants of the original red paint beneath the green can be seen on the side.

Don added a pine board to the side of an old black armchair to create a writing chair. The hanging box conceals a thermostat.

The small watercolor looks to be a New England or English piece with patriotic colors; Don estimates it dates to the early 20thC. He used an old ladderback to make the upholstered fireside chair. Don and Linda painted over the old wallpaper and then applied a Sherwin Williams paint called "Basket Weave" to create an aged look.

Linda found the hanging cupboard in Florida. The Pennsylvania long table dates to circa 1860 and is surrounded by a variety of ladderback chairs. The table is unique in that it features an end drawer which extends nearly the entire length of the table. Linda purchased the hanging lantern at the Hartville Flea Market for $5.

Linda painted pieces of Styrofoam fruit with a walnut colored stain to age them and subdue their color. The carrier at the end of the table holds early redware plates.

Don made the hanging buttery to display some of their crocks.

The oil on canvas over the faux mantel was found in Pennsylvania, while the large shelves display Don and Linda's pewter collection. The large charger on the top shelf was found on eBay®.

Atop the gray pie safe, the red paint decorated box was found in a Tennessee shop tucked under a table. Don and Linda purchased the box for $10 and brought it to a restoration expert in Pennsylvania who dated it to the late 1700's.

Many pieces of salt-glazed stoneware in Don and Linda's collection are native to Mogador and its vicinity, like those seen on the small bucket bench under the window.

Linda used old linen for her window treatments.

An old yellowware batter bowl and mortar and pestle rest on top of a dry sink with attic surface. Some of Linda's tin cookie cutters are displayed in the small trencher in the back.

Linda cooks on the old gas stove dating to the turn of the century.

The mustard cup with blind doors is from Ohio; remnants of original red paint can be seen upon close inspection under the mustard. An old winnowing board sits on top of the early blue painted store counter which Linda uses as an island.

Don used more of his salvaged wood to build shelves beside the brick chimney; Linda uses the space to display jars of spices and dried herbs. The stoneware butter churn with a salt glazed flower pattern is a Mogador piece.

Linda and Don often use their enclosed porch off the kitchen for summer suppers. The yellow hanging cupboard seen right came from a log cabin; it hangs over what appears to be a bucket bench but is actually a dry sink with holes cut in the top to create a sieve. It was found in North Carolina.

Linda found the early blue cupboard in Florida and treats it with kid gloves. The old red cupboard was found in Michigan in someone's trash. The shelves on top are old tin spice cans.

Jeanette Mosier of Ohio painted the
Rufus Porter style mural featuring George
Washington.

A period bedroom off the living room
features a small portrait which is actually a
color print put on canvas of a friend's great-
great grandmother. Don painted the floor cloth.

The lift-top table in early red wash was found in Ohio. The wall behind the faux fireplace is a fake wall added by Don to conceal wires and equipment.

Don and Linda hung the small corner cupboard high to keep the children from eating all the jam that was stored inside. The ladder provides access to adults only!

Don made the decoy on the mantel. Additional decoys are displayed in the cupboard to the right of the mantel.

Don and Linda's backyard garden is another artistic arrangement, most of the pieces created by Don from salvaged materials. The open latticed structure at the center of the garden holds a swing.

Don and Linda used iron bars fashioned by local blacksmith Kim Thomas, adding gourds to create an imaginative fence.

Don and Linda use the fire pit often. Below, a rusted bike is used to create another imaginative fence.

Notice the chain suspended from the overhang of the shed. Adopted from the Amish, rainwater for the gardens trickles down the chain and collects in a bucket below.

Don and Linda rent booth space at the Seville Antique Center; their Website is www.sevilleantiques.com. Don makes numerous items which he sells, and may be contacted at 330-221-9864.

Chapter 5

❖

Sharyn and Lloyd Sheats

A sweeping porch across the entire front of the house provides a tranquil setting on summer evenings.

Sharyn and Lloyd Sheats have been married 45 years and spent over 30 years as dairy farmers in Delaware. The Sheats lived on the main farm until eight years ago when Lloyd and Sharyn moved into their present home. Although Lloyd still grows corn and beans with his brother, he manages to find time to antique with Sharyn and add to their extensive collection of decoys, weathervanes, and stoneware.

Sharyn and Lloyd met in high school and started collecting antiques early in their marriage, preferring to strip pieces down to an attic finish, as many of us did. Fifteen years ago, they started collecting pieces with original painted surfaces and have been slowly replacing their initial purchases.

Despite a dry spell in late summer, the backyard garden still radiated color. The blue hanging birdhouses provided striking contrast against the cluster of yellow lilies.

The kitchen extends across the back of the house and includes a gathering area with a fireplace. The kitchen is painted with "Rittenhouse Green" and "Valley Forge Mustard" from Old Village Paints.

The early hanging plate rack in green paint holds some of Sharyn and Lloyd's pewter collection. An early cow weathervane rests in the well of a bucket bench in dry blue paint. Three unique stoneware pieces from Sharyn's collection fill the bottom shelf. Sharyn typically selects stoneware pieces with salt-glazed animals and rare figures. The crock depicting a pair of birds is Norton from Bennington, Vermont, as is the crock alongside picturing a deer.

The 19thC red crock cupboard was found during Lloyd and Sharyn's first trip to the Heart of Country Antique Show in Nashville, Tennessee, in 2000. Sharyn and Lloyd saw this same cupboard 35 years earlier in a shop, but with three small children and a new business, they couldn't justify the purchase. They were shocked to find it at Heart of Country and didn't hesitate to bring it home. More prize crocks fill the cupboard; top row left to right is shown an unsigned "jug on crock", a lion by the Farrar Co. in Geddes, New York, and a flower pot design by Clark in Lyons, New York. Bottom shelf middle is pictured a unique three chickens pecking corn, and far right a disproportionate bird in a nest in a tree. On top of the cupboard sits a large cow weathervane, a special reminder of Lloyd and Sharyn's previous lives as dairy farmers.

A small apothecary with mustard paint was found in Maryland. A collection of baskets and crocks adorns the top of the cupboard.

Three weathervanes rest on a painted bucket bench in the kitchen: a rare calf by E. G. Washburne & Co., a Blackhawk Horse, and a small rooster. More stoneware salt glazed crocks line the bottom shelf.

A signed Jewell & Co. horse jumping through a hoop weathervane rests on a red painted sideboard table. A collection of firkins in original paint is clustered beneath the table, while a small stack of painted pantry boxes sits to the right. Note the stack of wonderful miniature painted boxes.

A small stepback cupboard in wonderful dry blue paint displays a Marino Ram weathervane by Cushing & Co.

Lloyd's collection of decoys, found at shows and purchased privately from collectors, is striking. A regal James Holly goose rests atop an early pine corner cupboard.

The painting above the mantel depicts a pair of Madison Mitchell canvasbacks. Beneath it, a Ward Brothers Bishop-Head goose rests beside a grasshopper weathervane.

Tucked in the corner, a small blue cupboard is filled with stoneware crocks. An early peg rack holds early painted dough bowls and a trencher.

A dated 1830 sampler hangs above a bucket bench filled with some of Lloyd's decoy collection.

Sharyn and Lloyd found the 57-drawer stepback apothecary in Massachusetts; it retains its original mustard paint. Standing on the top is a bull weathervane by Cushing & Co. Sharyn and Lloyd couldn't resist the early "Milk 30 cents a gal." sign over the doorway.

A collection of miniature decoys carved in the Mason style by Louis Scheyd of New Hampshire is displayed in a pine divided box with lovely patina.

The Sheats added the sunroom at the back of the house in 2003. A large stag weathervane, attributed to Cushing & Co, sits atop a blue painted apothecary and creates a spectacular silhouette. Across the top of the large window and above the "Crockery & Glassware" sign, a shelf holds a collection of stoneware churns.

A rare Charlie Joiner full-size swan sits on top of a mule chest with early blue paint.

The trim paint in the sunroom is "Antique Pewter" by Old Village Paints.

A collection of early geese from various carvers sits on a shelf in the sunroom, while a collection of graduated pewter chargers provides a striking backdrop for the geese.

The 19thC blind door cupboard with green paint holds early Ward Brothers decoys.

An early horse and sulky weathervane sits in the well of an early painted bucket bench with red paint. The bottom shelves hold an assortment of cake crocks from the mid-Atlantic region.

Assorted pieces of Flow Blue fill the red painted early stepback found in Virginia.

A Samuel L. Plank wall box hangs to the right of the fireplace. Plank lived near Allenville, Pennsylvania in Mifflin County. The gameboard is early. The jug on the mantel is a signed Cowden Wilcox from Harrisburg, Pennsylvania, depicting "the man in the moon". The large painting is done in the Alfred Montgomery style.

An Indian weathervane of St. Tammany of the Delaware tribe stands atop a Delaware blanket chest in blue paint.

The blue painted cupboard found in Maryland provides an ideal space to display unique stoneware. The cupboard's blue blends beautifully with the cobalt stoneware.

Three shorebirds, two by Ward Brothers and one contemporary shorebird by Bill Gibbeon, stand on top.

A large horse weathervane appears to race across the top of a pewter cupboard filled with early English pewter. Sharyn and Lloyd found some of the pewter pieces during a trip to England and Scotland. A graduated stack of early painted firkins stands to the right.

A 19thC bucket bench with early red paint holds a set of graduated stoneware crocks from Baltimore, while the bottom shelf holds a collection of early English pewter. An early painted gameboard hangs above the bench.

A stack of 15 early pantry boxes in a variety of painted colors stands in the corner beside a mustard tilt-top stenciled table. A dated 1839 Pennsylvania coverlet drapes over the back of the table.

A bucket bench in original blue holds a large collection of pewter spoons and chargers. A variety of uniquely shaped stoneware pitchers, jugs, and lidded cake crocks fills three shelves.

A large grouping of early painted gameboards decorates the stairway in the foyer.

Sharyn and Lloyd found the circa 1940's hooked rug at a show in Pennsylvania; the subject matter made it irresistible.

A small table in the foyer holds an early Ward Brothers black duck, old blue lantern, and pewter plate. A grouping of stoneware can be seen under the table. The early Parcheesi gameboard is shown in Tim Chambers's book entitled, "The Art of the Game".

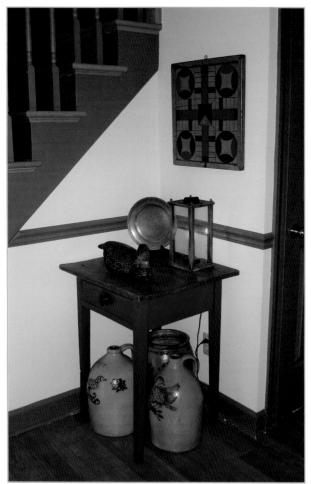

A Pennsylvania heart pine stepback features a 24-pane glass top and holds a 24 place setting of Austrian Haviland from Sharyn's mother.

Six mustard paint decorated Pennsylvania chairs surround the early farm table; a Cushing & Co. pig weathervane sits in the center. The mustard painted corner cupboard is filled with a collection of Flow Blue.

I was immediately drawn to the small cupboard with hooded back in wonderful blue paint; it holds three pewter plates and an early large red trencher. A pair of early Charlie Joiner teal stands on top. The early spoon rack above holds a large collection of pewter spoons.

The weathervane in front of the window is a "Ranger" by Cushing & White. It stands on a Virginia tavern table in magnificent dry bittersweet paint.

Sharyn and Lloyd found the red over green painted crock cupboard in Tennessee and have filled it with stoneware from various regions.

A Pennsylvania server with original putty paint holds a collection of early black ducks by various carvers.

An early blue trencher in original paint hangs on a peg rack over Ward Brothers miniature decoys.

A miniature pair of Elmer Crowell mallards is displayed among a collection of black ducks.

A large Baltimore 2-gallon stoneware pitcher sits atop a blue splay-legged table. A crock with a starface from T. Harrington, Lyons, New York, stands on the floor beside two others depicting a lady holding an umbrella and another with a willow tree.

Sharyn and Lloyd's collections are extraordinary and clearly museum quality. Each is unique, tastefully displayed as one might find in a museum, yet warm and welcoming.

Chapter 6

^ ✿ ^

Candace and Bob Littiken

Before Bob and Candace were married 18 years ago, Bob collected general store memorabilia such as Coca-Cola and gas station signs. Then he and Candace traveled to Williamsburg, Virginia, came home, and sold everything in their house to various friends who were antique dealers. Bob and Candace built the home where they currently live in 2001 in Hebron, Indiana, having moved from a small house in a neighboring town. Bob acted as the general contractor, and did as much of the work as possible himself such as interior trim, floors, and painting. The blueprints for the center chimney saltbox were modified by McKie Roth from Maine, who measured old houses and then redrew blueprints to scale. The Littiken's house is historically true to form, as the ceilings on both floors are 7'8" rather than the traditional 8' ceilings upstairs. Bob works part-time as a custodian at a local church having retired as owner of the Indiana Tent Cleaning Company.

The house has cedar siding and is painted with Olde Century "Barn Red" paint. The gutters are copper; the roof is cedar shakes. Bob and Candace spent four years searching and collecting artifacts, such as the front steps that came from a Pennsylvania house.

The Littiken's home has been on the local garden tour twice. When I asked who the gardener was, Bob responded that their entire house is comprised of "we". The front yard is a "dooryard garden", so named because the produce was grown close to the door and handy for picking. Bob and Candace raise 30 different herb varieties and supply or trade herbs with a local restaurant.

Bob bought the wonderful blue bucket at a church sale. The sundial in the background rests on an early architectural piece found at a garage sale.

The potted geraniums against the weathered fence caught my eye.

What a unique way to display birdhouses! I'm looking forward to spring when I can do the same.

The hanging window provides a wonderful portal to the yard; many of the 525 visitors on the garden tour marveled at the illusion it creates.

Bob and Candace found the fencing sections at Lowes. The gate which Bob says "goes nowhere" was made from an old door he cut down.

The cricket table in the center of the Keeping Room is pegged and features a Spanish brown-painted top. A pewter bowl rests on top. The solid standing six-board chest was purchased at Ginny Curry Antiques in Lancaster, Ohio; it retains its original green paint.

The mustard cupboard found in southern Indiana was a housewarming gift from Bob to Candace. It features early blue paint, scalloped shelving, and ball feet. A collection of brushed Flow Blue is displayed, along with an onion ware plate on the top shelf. My eye was immediately drawn to the horizontal chamfered piece in front- a small drawer. The Windsor chair with salmon paint was purchased at Four Chimneys Antiques in Mainville, Ohio.

The stepback seen left was found in southern Indiana. Bob and Candace attended a farm auction where white ironstone was being sold; they bid $26 and were the winners of 42 pieces that now fill the cupboard. The basket on top is an authentic Shaker basket.

The early red cupboard at the far end of the room is a Pennsylvania piece. The oval box on the middle shelf is an early bride's box, most likely Scandinavian.

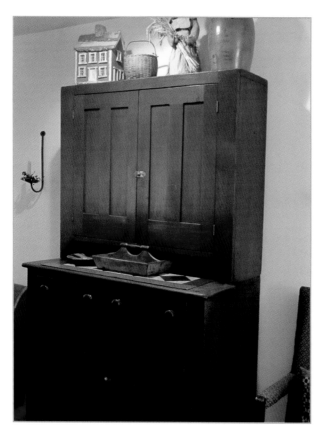

A graduated stack of painted sugar buckets stands beside an early child's sled. The wall box is an old saltbox from Maine.

The trim paint is Olde Century "Olde Ivory". Bob met a dealer who many years ago had disassembled a home and saved the mantel, seen above. A hunt board to the left of the Rumford fireplace holds early utensils.

The musket above the fireplace was a gift from a friend. An early pewter oil lamp rests on the mantel beneath it. The pewter chargers are English.

An early buttocks basket rests on a unique server with original green and red paint. The small server was found in Waynesville, Ohio. The portrait was found in Michigan at an antiques yard sale.

Bob and Candace have since replaced the sawbuck table, a Sally Whims' piece, with an early table. The chairs are from David T. Smith.

The lines on the early ladderback are exceptional. The still life was found at the Richmond Show held in June and October.

A sugar cone and nippers sit on top of a unique cant back bucket bench in salmon paint.

The long church pew came from an Episcopal church in Kentucky. There is a mouse hole behind the basket on the left, which Bob says their grandson loves to drop his toys through.

A small table fits perfectly inside the door. Bob and Candace found their all grain-painted front door on a trip to Williamsburg in a small town called Ordinary, Virginia.

The tall clock in the front hall belonged to Bob's mother. The corner cupboard is from Pennsylvania and holds a large collection of mainly European pewter, half of which Bob found on ebay®.

Candace utilized her 20 years experience as a kitchen designer to create a functional but beautiful kitchen. Bob made the free- standing unit used as an island from an old red cupboard.

The counters and sink are Vermont soapstone. The slant top desk hides a telephone.

The dining area off the kitchen is painted with Olde Century "Cupboard Blue". The drop-leaf table is early and features a "company" board which can be added to extend the table-which convinced Bob and Candace that, despite the price, it was a must have. The table has a scrub top and attic finish base.

Bob and Candace found the old floor cloth at Davie's Auctions in Lafayette, Indiana.

Bob and Candace found the 19thC dry sink with gray/green paint in Kentucky. The make-do spoon rack is constructed with the base of a mallet and old butter paddle turned upside down.

The Tavern Room is painted with Olde Century "Bittersweet" paint. A green onion bottle rests on a Connecticut tavern table dating to the late 18thC. The hutch table seen below is a ship captain's table found in New York. The large stepback at the back holds an early large basket on top. The Windsor chair is a new piece. A corner wall shelf holds a collection of early whiskey jugs, many that feature writing, dating to the early 1900's and found in Kentucky and Ohio.

Vintage tins are displayed along with an early cape and tricorn hat. The red and black gameboard resting against the wall is early.

The Littiken's use the grain painted wall cupboard above the commode as a medicine cabinet.

The cupboard on the landing at the top of the stairs is 6' wide and was a challenge to get upstairs; it serves as a bookcase and holds a mantel clock, basket, and leather bound books on top. The ladderback chairs are early and strategically placed so no one sits in them. One chair holds an authentic Shaker bonnet. The candle shelf beside it has an old tin make-do repair and is joined with dovetails.

A barely visible trundle bed provides extra space in the smaller of the two bedrooms. The quilt at the foot of the bed is one of 29 made by Bob's mother.

A child's desk holds a small doll chair and early inkwell and quill pen. The trim paint in this room is Olde Century "Old Brick Red".

Bob's mother participated in weekend festivals and dressed in period clothing; a few of her period dresses are displayed in the alcove. All of the door thumb latches were fashioned by a blacksmith in nearby Conner Prairie.

The two-door kas was found in Illinois and retains its original black paint.

A chest with glove boxes on top may be poplar and has lovely tones, as each drawer features a slightly different hue.

The blue and tan linen coverlets on the master bedroom beds were found at Ginny Curry Antiques in Lancaster, Ohio. More of Bob's mother's antique quilts are folded on top of early chests at the foot of the beds.

The blue and red coverlet displayed on the quilt rack is a signed Ohio piece.

The corner cupboard is pegged and has a removable scrolled top piece, perhaps to accommodate a low ceiling. It was found at the Richmond Show.

A sampler found at Heart of Country in Nashville hangs above a Rumford fireplace in the master bedroom. The mantel is painted with "Leather Bound Book Brown" from TruValue Hardware. The early mantel was found at Miller House Antiques in Carroll, Ohio.

A signed rope bed tightener is displayed on a peg rack with red, white, and blue vintage clothing.

The table and chairs on the back porch are made of old Indiana hickory.

Bob and Candace's 2100 square foot home is located one hour from Chicago. They have decided to downsize and have placed their home on the market. The property may still be for sale. If interested, the Littikens may be reached via email at saltbox01@hotmail.com.

Chapter 7

Ed Oestreich

Ed Oestreich, a retired Lutheran pastor from Pennsylvania, vacationed on the Pemaquid Peninsula of Maine for 20 years prior to his retirement and permanent move to an old home in Damariscotta, Maine. A collector of fine antiques for over 50 years, Ed felt that the late 18thC home was ideal; it had been kept intact by its previous owners down to the earth floor in the basement. Ed chose the exterior California house paint,

"Portsmouth Spice", after Consumers Guide rated it best for long-lasting durability. Ed chose the paint to duplicate the color of an 18thC house in Portsmouth, New Hampshire. The original house consisted of just two rooms-the formal parlor and the multi-purpose kitchen that featured a buttery. The Great Room was added in the mid 1900's.

A visitor enters the summer kitchen, added in the 19thC, through a fully double-battened door from an early 18thC house in Topsham, Maine. Ed installed a rare, late 17thC wrought iron knocker which serves also as a locking latch. Ed found the granite post, circa 1850, in Maine; it retains its original iron hitching ring.

Standing in the center of Ed's Great Room is a Pennsylvania refectory table. Made of black walnut, it has been authenticated to 1690-1710 by Winterthur. An early ladderback in red wash with original mushroom handholds is seen at the near end. The arm chair in original black paint with sloping arms is a New England piece dating to the early 1700's.

Dyes date the pre-1870's Oriental rug folded at the end of the table to circa 1870. An oval maple chopping bowl in blue paint was found in nearby Edgecomb, Maine, and is one of Ed's favorite pieces. I found the 18thC burl beehive bowl beside it, also in blue, to be my favorite.

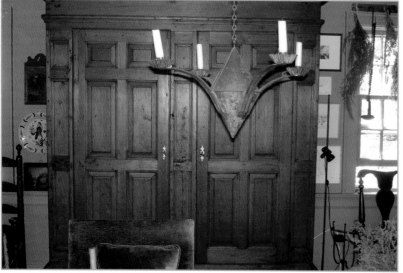

The gate leg table, made of Yew wood, is English and dates to the mid 17thC.

The 18thC New England slant top desk with attic surface was most likely a reading or store counter desk. Ed has filled the desk with leather-bound 18thC store ledgers that he has collected over the years. Several 18thC "Case" gin bottles, an early blown wine bottle, and two 17thC blown wine glasses are stashed inside to refresh the bookkeeper!

The large piece seen left is a Pennsylvania "schrank" (pronounced schronk). Similar storage pieces were used, as closets were rarely found in 18thC homes. The Holland Dutch would refer to this piece as a kas. Ed purchased the schrank from early mentors Jack and Lucy Lamb, who found the piece outside a barn in Pennsylvania where it was used to store chicken feed. Apparently each time the farmer painted the barn, he applied another coat of paint to the schrank. Ms. Lamb worked for over a year to remove the layers of paint. At the time, Ed thought the $700 he paid the Lamb's was a great deal of money. The schrank features raised-panel doors and sunken panels on the sides. The hinges are rat tail hinges allowing for easy removal of the doors for transport. Inside, a top shelf with oval opening is called a bonnet shelf. The tin chandelier hanging in front dates to about 1800.

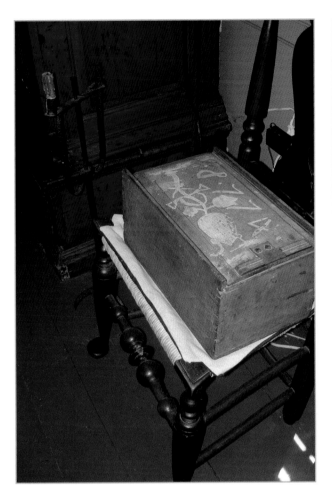

A 17thC New England linen-fold chest, named for its shadow molding, retains its original red wash. A Hudson River chair beside it holds a paint decorated and dated 1774 Pennsylvania candlebox, acquired from the Paul Flack collection. The New England hanging pewter shelf dates to the 18thC and was purchased from Peter Tillou of Litchfield, Connecticut. The deep dish on the third shelf from the bottom at the far right is dated 1792 and belonged to Henry Francis DuPont.

The birch desk with case, right, was found in nearby Westbrook, Maine, and is completely original and untouched. The New England roundabout chair dates to the 18thC and is placed in front of the desk, where early inventories, taken in rooms after an owner passed away, indicates this as the usual position of such chairs.

The tiny bottle in one desk cubby was excavated in Jerusalem by a biblical archeologist. Most likely used for perfume or ointment, the Roman bottle dates to the 1st century, CE. The glass is iridescent from centuries of being buried under sand. The larger bottle is English and dates to the early 18thC; it was retrieved from a riverbed in the American colonies. The horn comb is the same that George Newmann illustrated in his book, "Early American Country Furnishings", and dates to the 18thC. The triangular-shaped piece is an American magnifying glass or prism made around 1800. A small wooden plug on one side could be removed to allow the glass-sided device to be filled with water. Placed over any reading material, the prism enlarged the print; it retains its original mustard paint.

Tucked in the corner, a circa 1730 chest in original black paint was made in York, Maine. On it stands a Dutch Delft plate, purchased by Ed because of the early 18thC metal staple repairs visible on the back. A child's bonnet, probably French circa 1730 and employing silk embroidery and silver metallic thread, rests next to the Delft. The looking glass above is Continental and 17thC.

The Pennsylvania stepback at the opposite end of the room dates to 1810-1820. On top is a pair of Pennsylvania 19thC, recumbent chalk deer. The upper shelves hold theological leather-bound books which belonged to Ed's grandfather, also a Lutheran pastor. The pair of hand-painted Chinese Export oval serving dishes on the bottom shelf was part of a complete service ordered by Captain John Paul Jones when he outfitted his sloop of war, Ranger, out of Portsmouth, New Hampshire, during the War for Independence.

The circa 1770 paneled chest, seen right, retains its original blue paint. It is a Hudson River Valley piece which Ed acquired from the collections of Historic Deerfield, after they deaccessioned some of their non-Connecticut River Valley furniture. The two portraits above date to the first quarter of the 19thC; the names of the Connecticut couple are painted on the back.

The 18thC, redware deep bowl from Pennsylvania is decorated with a human figure which, according to Joe Kindig, a leading authority on Pennsylvania redware, makes it a very rare piece. The late 18th/ early 19thC hexagonal table rug beneath is a hooked and sheared piece and, based on its colors, believed to have been made in Maine.

Bronze spoon molds for making pewter spoons are displayed at the right side of the chest. The largest mold, seen at the rear, bears a profile-portrait engraving, a commemoration of Queen Anne's coronation in 1702. The carved wooden figure, perhaps Italian, is probably St. Francis and dates to the late 17thC.

The William & Mary courting mirror is Continental. The portraits beneath, framed in the original lemon gilt, are Dutch. Ed found the 18thC penmanship work, used most likely as a bookmark, in one of his grandfather's books; it translates from the Pennsylvania German dialect to read, "Remembrances of Youth".

An 18thC American adjustable tin floor-standing lighting device carries double candle sockets. For stability, the conical base was filled with sand. Behind it on the table stands a scarce early English bottle, rare because of its half bottle size. Partially visible behind a salt glaze jug rests a 17thC yellow ceramic candlestick, excavated and restored in Holland.

The cut velvet waistcoat dates to circa 1730. The original wearer, John Leverett, inked his name inside the linen back; if lost or stolen the owner could be identified. Leverett, a grandson of one of the last royal governors of Massachusetts, was president of Harvard.

Interesting pieces are displayed surrounding the mantel in the little parlor. Although the sitter in the center portrait is identified, it is unsigned but probably Dutch or American. On either side of this portrait hang two family records; one for the wedding of a Revolutionary War officer from Maine, the other for their children's births and deaths. A tiny black-glass recumbent dog was probably the lid finial of a Wedgewood tureen.

The watercolor of Mrs. Joseph Wood was painted by noted Pennsylvania artist Jacob Mantel in the early 19thC. Beneath it, a water color miniature in its original frame with inscriptions on the back is signed by Anna Claypoole Peale of the famed Peale family of artists. An 18thC Revolutionary War soldier, Peter Comstock II of Montville, Connecticut, born July 11, 1731, is the sitter. Although unsigned, the profile portrait in the original frame is attributed to Rufus Porter because three of Porter's characteristic features have been identified.

A delightful 19thC carved yellowbird stands beneath the framed title page from the 18thC book, "Voyages of Captain Cook". At either end of the mantel stand rare American candlesticks.

An 18thC hanging watch hutch holds a timepiece that belonged to Ed's grandfather. Above it, an 18thC Pennsylvania wrought iron keyhole escutcheon in the shape of a cockerel creates an interesting pattern against the white wall.

A child's shirt is early 19thC and hangs above an 18thC pair of children's shoes. The blacksmith anvil is one of only three* known to have come from the original Saugus Iron Works in Massachusetts. The brass bed warmer is engraved with the profile of the "not too attractive" Queen Anne.

The horn seen left is called a spill horn, so named because it holds spills, twisted paper, or shavings. Spills were used to light the pipe or another fireplace. Found behind a wall during the restoration of one of the earliest houses in Ipswich, Massachusetts, it is carve-decorated with a raised heart, initials, wavy lines, and dated 1735.

The corner cupboard was removed from an 18thC house in Massachusetts and retains its original blue-green paint. The shaped shelves hold a large collection of Salopian, English ceramic tableware made 1790-1820, exclusively for the American market. Over 150 patterns of this transfer ware have been identified. Ed's favorite pieces are those with pastoral scenes. The tall piece, fourth shelf from the top is called a veilleuse-a tea warmer, also called a night nurse, and considered the rarest example of Salopian. It would have been placed at the bedside of a sick person as a "night light" and to keep tea warm.

Purchased from Jack and Lucy Lamb, the bride's box on top of the cupboard was identified by the Lambs as Pennsylvania Dutch based on the clothing depicted and remnants of what appears to be an inscription in the Pennsylvania Dutch dialect.

On the floor is a rare metal couvre feu dating to the late 17thC. A safety ordinance was passed requiring homeowners to cover their fireplace at night to prevent sparks from starting a house fire. The French translates to "cover fire" from which we derive our word "curfew".

The circa 1730 highboy in the corner was made in Shirley, Massachusetts; it retains an untouched surface and original engraved brass English hardware. It descended in the same family and was found with two silhouette portraits of the family in one of the drawers.

The American 17thC Bible Box on top is from the well-known collection of the late Ignatius Weise; it is carved and retains its original red wash. A dated 1523 Jerome Bible lies next to it under an indenture written in the opening reign of Queen Anne.

A hanging pipe rack with original paint, circa 1800, was found in coastal Maine. The two pipes were salvaged from an early 19thC shipwreck off the coast of Florida. The portrait depicts a Maine sea captain, lost at sea at age 32. The back of the portrait is covered with a page from the ship's log.

A Connecticut worktable in original red wash with cutout corners, splay legs, and button feet stands in the middle of the room. An 18thC engraved glass tankard and a deck of hand-colored Tarot cards have been placed on it. The pocketbook belonged to Ichabod Jones and is dated 1767 within the needle worked design, along with his name. Researching Ichabod Jones, Ed discovered he was a detested Tory, a ship owner and captain from Boston with a mansion in Machias, Maine. In the winter of 1776, the British encamped in Boston and desperately needed wood, while the starving patriots in Machias needed food. Loading his ship with barrels of food, Jones sailed to Machias willing to exchange his cargo of food for the abundant Maine timbers. His plan failed when the patriots forced him to flee without the supplies . . . or the wood. Chasing him out to sea, the patriots fired on his ship, and so was fought the first naval battle of the Revolution. Jones managed to escape but his valuable Machias estate was confiscated by the Sons of Liberty.

The Pennsylvania table in blue-green paint is 18thC and was purchased from a North Carolina collection. Although described as a candlestand, it seems likely that the deep char in the center was caused by hot embers from a warming device. Ed believes it was actually a kettle stand. Given this interpretation, he displays a 17thC Dutch chafing dish and an 18thC Dutch kettle.

The young gentleman's silk embroidered vest is French and dates to circa 1800. It hangs in front of an 18thC woolen coat that retains its silver-thread buttons.

Ed couldn't resist the weather-worn painted surface of the pair of 18thC exterior shutters. A small Pennsylvania corner cupboard in original paint hangs in the corner. Beneath rests an English William & Mary period wing chair.

The candlestand seen left is a rare New England 18thC survivor in original surface featuring an octagonal lipped top. The elaborately turned shaft makes it quite unusual. The well-worn Bible, dated 1743, is Dutch.

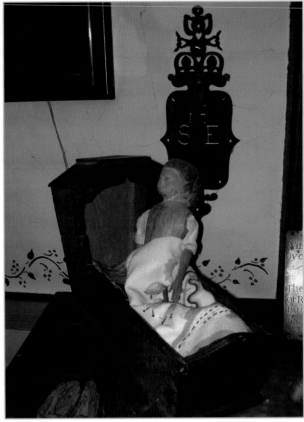

The ball foot, single arch molded blanket chest dates to the first decade of the 18thC. Its history is known, having been taken from an 18thC house in Massachusetts for which it was made.

The brass tomb plate records the deaths of two boys: William, 26, died in 1735, and Henry, 13, in 1747. Such plates were attached to a casket or grave marker. The plate records that while the boys shared their last name, their fathers' first names were different; this suggests that their widowed mother married her first husband's brother-a common 18thC practice.

While Ed collects early pieces, he also collects Christmas ornaments and toys from the Victorian period, such as the pecking hen toy pictured. He was drawn to this piece by its unusually detailed paint decoration. Although similar toys of Pennsylvania origin are recorded, this is probably German.

The early doll's cradle in blue-green paint found in a New Hampshire attic is considered by many as a finer example than those in the collections of Williamsburg or Winterthur. A vintage pair of shoes rests beside it. Although Ed tries to display pieces showing their original use, the New England 18thC door latch with elaborate cutouts begged to be displayed against a background which showcased its detail. The latch would have been used on a private home and bears the initials "S & E", with a surname beginning with "H".

A hat mold holds an early 1800's mob cap.

The American tin sconce is early 19thC and features a removable oval reflector. The framed document below, dated 1805, is a certificate stating the rental fee paid for the family church pew in Salem, Massachusetts. The top of an 18thC lamp lighter or torch came from the collection of a founder of the Rush Light Club.

Ed often was asked to act as chaplain on luxury cruises aboard ships of the Swedish-American Line, resulting in his visiting more than 50 countries. The small pencil sketch, shown top, was purchased in Denmark, and the woman's silhouette in Ireland. Both items date to the mid-19thC.

A small "parson's cupboard" in the front entrance holds a collection of bottles. Most notable on the top shelf, a pair of 18thC pharmaceutical bottles bears the owner's applied glass seal, "J.A. Willink". Ed learned that Willink was head of the bank in Amsterdam, from which the infant United States received its first loan. James Madison, Alexander Hamilton, and Thomas Jefferson patronized this bank. The collection of Historic Deerfield contains an identical pair of bottles. The bronze mortar is dated 1661.

The New England hanging wall box dates to the late 17thC; it is one of the best Ed has seen and retains much of its original red and black paint in the carving. Ed and the box crossed paths a number of times at auctions and dealers before Ed was finally able to acquire it.

A late 18thC rope bed in original blue paint is shown in the original kitchen.

A late 18thC lantern with shaved horn, a forerunner of glass, hangs in the window. The unsigned portrait was found in an Amherst, Massachusetts attic.

An early red quilted petticoat hangs beneath an 1800's Continental utensil rack filled with American wrought iron utensils; one features a brass inset dated 1811.

An 18thC candlestand purchased from Lillian Blankley Cogan of Connecticut holds two pair of 18thC wrought iron shears and an embossed 17thC scissors case. On the floor is a French watering can identical to one at Mt. Vernon.

A dated 1749 English engraving depicting the Battle of Drumossie Moor hangs over the mantel. Such engravings were made in England, sent to the colonies to be framed, and hung over a mantel. The engraving's legend identifies all the figures shown in this hand-colored scene.

The chair on the hearth is a Pilgrim century New England chair, as are two other chairs in this early room. The armchair in original black originated in North Shore, Massachusetts, and dates to the 18thC.

The child's potty chair with original mustard paint was discovered in Maine; it is constructed with rosehead nails and features a Queen Anne crest and skirt cutouts. The chair is one of Ed's favorite pieces, as it is an all-original child's chair made in the 17thC at Plimoth Plantation.

A tole-painted tea caddy stands on the mantel beside a framed Pennsylvania watercolor. Above, a framed Pennsylvania book plate belonging to Jacob Landau and dated 1848 is illuminated with numerous birds; the Landau family founded the museum that bears its name. A rare, leather costrel, used to carry rum or hard cider, hangs below.

Ed purchased the tin candlebox with original blue paint because of the seldom seen shield- shaped back. Ed still uses the cookie cutters on the mantel for holiday baking; they belonged to Ed's grandmother.

The child's bonnet was made by Mrs. Moses Dunston, wife of Revolutionary War officer Moses. The bonnet's origin was discovered from a handwritten "granny note" that accompanied it. Granny notes are inscriptions found on backing boards and attached to frames, frequently added by elderly relatives. Ed sold other items belonging to Mrs. Dunston, including her wedding slippers, which are now at Deerfield.

Both tankards are rare early 18thC New England pieces. The one on the right in original blue paint is New Hampshire; it is so out-of-round that the base is oval! The larger of the two was found in Maine. The chalk portrait, although unsigned, is stylistically similar and attributed to portraits by Benjamin Blyth.

A small, 18thC American hanging corner cupboard holds a collection of pottery. The footed clay pot on the bottom shelf was excavated in Holland in a field where, during the bubonic plague, bodies and household items were thrown into a common grave. Three jugs with a bearded man face on the front, usually referred to as Bellarmine jugs, are displayed. Bellarmine was actually a Cardinal, dreaded by the Protestants. Interestingly, when the first bearded jug was made, Bellarmine was only eight years of age! These bearded jugs are better called, as in England, "bartmann krug", German for bearded man jug.

The oval top 18thC table is actually a hutch table. The surface is marvelous! While in the home of an earlier owner, the table was featured in an old issue of "The Magazine Antiques". A tiny 18thC iron, used to press ruffles, lace, or ribbons, sits on a fabric remnant at one end.

A magnificent 18thC glass carboy, blown into a mold, stands regally at the end of a lift top chest. The chest, which features ball feet and original red wash, retains its original snipe hinges and dates to circa 1720. It is from the collection of John and Joan Thayer.

A rare American iron trammel, found at Almodington Plantation, Maryland, is scratch decorated and dated 1746. If extended to its full length, it would reach 7-8 feet! Note the fine upper blacksmith design. An elegant, paneled room from Almodington is installed at the Metropolitan Museum in New York City.

Ed purchased the 18thC blown bottle because of its perfect spherical body.

The bottle rests on what is commonly referred to as a hornbeam-named for the tree-although this piece is not made of that wood. This example is a hollowed-out tree trunk, circa 18thC, featuring iron hoops added later to prevent splitting.

The hanging 18thC cupboard seen left is Pennsylvania and retains its original hinges, escutcheon, and key. A large 18thC birch beehive bowl with traces of original red paint rests on top.

Seen above left, a rare corner dresser in original blue-green paint was removed from a house in northern Maine. The paint is perfectly preserved because both the walls and the ends of the dresser were papered. The dresser retains its original HL hinges and 17-step molding at top. Sealed bottles, crocks, pantry boxes, and firkins line the shelves. The eagle on the first shelf was carved by Aaron Mountz of Pennsylvania in the late 19thC. He learned the trade from folk artist Shimmel; unlike Schimmel, Mountz rarely painted his work. This is a rare example of a painted Mountz eagle. Schimmel died an alcoholic pauper in the alms house.

Ed restored the wall to accommodate the narrow chimney cupboard, which holds a collection of early pewter.

An 18thC New England lantern with replaced early glass hangs above a rare 18thC staved barrel constructed with rosehead nails and wooden pegs. Ed displays a pair of colorful striped mittens made on a small home loom and lined with early homespun.

A Revolutionary War camp stove, used to heat food, is unusual because of its heart-shaped shield which protected the user's hands when moving the stove.

Ed's gardens were lovely despite the fact that I arrived on the heels of a windy, rainy spell of weather. Nestled in the flowers, a large piece of quartz sparkles in the sunlight.

19thC ship's knees, used to help support the ship's deck, add an interesting architectural element to one section of the garden.

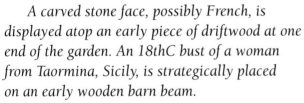

A carved stone face, possibly French, is displayed atop an early piece of driftwood at one end of the garden. An 18thC bust of a woman from Taormina, Sicily, is strategically placed on an early wooden barn beam.

Meeting Ed and photographing his home was truly a marvelous educational experience for me. Ed's collections and his knowledge of history speak to the value of research, the thrill of bringing the past alive, and the importance of sharing that knowledge and preserving our heritage.

Chapter 8

❧ ✾ ☙

Betty Jean and Jack Dalrymple

Often after filming a house, I come away with the memory of a distinct characteristic and a dominant overall theme of the home. Such was the case with Jack and Betty Jean Dalrymple's home in Delaware. You'll see what I mean! Jack and Betty Jean both grew up in New Jersey where Betty Jean was a primary grade school teacher and Jack an Instrumental Technician with a major oil company. In 2005, they began to build their retirement home in Delaware on land they had previously purchased. During the building phase, Jack and Betty Jean lived in an apartment and used the Delaware home as their weekend retreat. Betty Jean found the plans for the colonial on the internet after searching for a design that maximized the number of rooms while limited the home to 2400 square feet; a parameter they had decided would fit their financial plans. Retired now for four years, Betty Jean admits she has not been bored one day --and you'll see why! Wait till you see what she has hidden in the large storage area over the garage! Jack enjoys building

and woodworking and keeps busy with his hobbies and his church work.

The Dalrymples used Cabot's "Twilight Blue" stain on the outside of the house. A side entrance of stone adds texture and a nice contrast with the blue. Betty Jean enjoys gardening with flowers but not vegetables. There were beautiful impatiens planted the length of the long walk up to the door from the driveway. The back yard and patio were lovely as well - even through the pouring rain---but I was unable to capture them on film.

Jack made the shelf in the dining room to hold some of Betty Jean's large pewter collection. Notice the graduated assembled set of pewter porringers hanging from the bottom shelf. Betty Jean used to make items and sold them in a local gift shop. She admits she took nearly all of her profit out in pewter pieces from the shop. The drop leaf table belonged to Jack's grandmother. Betty Jean took a class in scherenschnitte and created the framed piece over the table.

Jack and Betty Jean had the Amish build their kitchen cabinets; the raised panel doors are attached with butterfly hinges. Betty Jean used a custom mixed paint in their kitchen. Her counter tops are Corian which she chose for the cost savings over soapstone and the ease of maintenance. She hasn't regretted her decision.

One of Betty Jean's talents is her ability to find reproductions that look so authentic one would never know they weren't the real thing. While she would love to own antiques, she admits their budget doesn't permit it. One example is the iron trivet on the counter. A wooden plate rack holds their everyday useable pewter called Wilton Armetale.

An herb cutter stands atop a small apothecary. The wax lamb above it is placed beside a new butter press. The iron lamb cake mold is old.

Three lidded stoneware crocks stand between two spice boxes purchased at a local country shop. The stoneware is called Maple City Pottery. Another lidded piece can be seen at the end of a shelf that Jack built over the stove. Three small yellowware custard cups were found at a local retail shop and are actually microwave and dishwasher safe.

Betty Jean displays her collection of candle molds above the refrigerator. Hanging from the beam are three old Betty Lamps. On the cupboard over the stove, coffee grinders, mashers and early tins fill the top.

An eating area on the back side of the kitchen was referred to by the builders as the "morning room" because of the wrap around windows and amount of sunlight.

Betty Jean found a wonderful collection
of painted muslin birds for $2 each which she
placed over the window and on the table. A
corn dryer with red apples is suspended from
a bucket bench under the window. More apples
fill the hanging scale. The pot belly stove isn't
activated but Betty Jean fills it with Christmas lights which
simulate an active fire. On the table, Betty Jean uses
a standing candlemold as a vase for tea dyed sunflowers.

Lots of old and new butter presses and molds are stacked
on a shelf. Graduated sets of Watt and yellowware bowls
can be seen on the other two shelves.

One of Betty Jean's exceptional talents is her rug hooking
ability. One such example is displayed over a jelly cupboard
that Jack built. The hanging tin cutters and the wonderful
board with heart cutout are two examples of Betty Jean's
ability to find replica pieces. The bowls were purchased at
a retail chain years ago when they were closing; Betty Jean
purchased all they had.

The floral hooked rug hanging in the side entranceway was the first Betty Jean ever hooked.

A bench beneath features a cover on the cushion of gray flannel to which Betty Jean sewed a penny rug.

Jack and Betty Jean had the builder use the "leftover" stone from the side entrance to create a fireplace surround. Betty Jean used a CharlesWysocki card to paint the fireboard.

The Jefferson writing chair in front was a gift to Betty Jean from Jack for her birthday. Jack made the cupboard on the left of the fireplace to hold their stereo equipment; he also built the settle on the right. Betty Jean has made over 150 samplers since the 1980's; she has given many away as gifts but displays others throughout the house. The sampler over the mantel was unfinished when she purchased it. It included the threads and was dated 2000. Betty Jean finished it and dated it 2009. She would like to know who started the sampler and hopes that person might read this chapter and contact her.

The calendar tacked to a breadboard end cutting board is in keeping with the period .

The cobbler's bench, used as a coffee table, is early as is the large spinning wheel behind the couch.

Jack built the dry sink beside the staircase; it holds a television. Betty Jean's samplers hang above it. She also made and designed the hanging hooked rug.

Above are three of the punch needle hooked small hangings Betty Jean has made. The sheep theme might give you a hint of her hidden space over the garage!

Betty Jean made the log cabin quilt in the upper left of the quilt rack in the guestroom.

A black Mammy rocking bench is at the foot of the bed in the master bedroom. Betty Jean found the blue and white coverlet years ago and has always liked the Williamsburg blue color.

Jack made the cradle in the corner in which all three of their children have slept. Betty Jean made the hooked rug over the wardrobe.

I thought Jack's idea of concealing the base of the tub was ingenious. The panel doors are in keeping with the décor while at the same time allow access to the plumbing below.

Betty Jean has displayed a number of "laundry items such as old irons, wringers, tins, and scrub boards in her second floor laundry room.

Betty Jean, an avid rug hooker for the past four years, converted the storage space over the garage into her own "cave". It is filled <u>everywhere</u> with sewing and rug hooking related items-a real delight to a fellow rug hooker. An early baker's rack on the right holds wool ready for hooking. Betty Jean buys 98% of her wool from Goodwill Industries. She uses the school desk as her cutting board. Suspended from the ceiling is a collection of early niddy noddys.

Jack made the green cupboard, shown above, that now displays fabric covered pantry boxes on top, an early sewing machine and an array of pin cushions. I particularly like the cushions in the early woman's shoes. Betty Jean used another corn dryer to display early bobbins with a variety of colored threads. The blue piece on the side of the cupboard is a spoon rack which Betty Jean uses to hold antique rug hooks. Other early sewing shears create a nice pattern against the wall.

Spools of thread hang from an old corn dryer. A tool box insert holds some of Betty Jean's collection of sheep. The sheep hooked rug was adapted from an antique pattern.

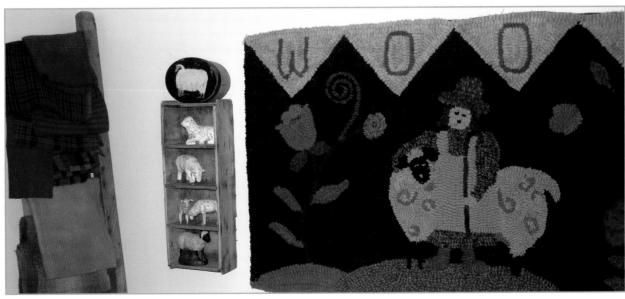

A shelf holds sheep of every size and color, a redware plate with a sheep design, baskets, flax, and embroidery hoops.

Betty Jean designed and hooked the 'wool gatherer' rug hanging beside a small wooden box holding wool squares. An early shuttle provides a shelf for small sheep.

Seen left, part of an early derby hat form becomes the perfect round frame for one of Betty Jean's wooly sheep pictures. Betty Jean wound red, green and tan yarn around the three early yarn winders she owns.

Trunk inserts provide ideal display shelves for Betty Jean's sheep. The small shelf holds spools of threads as does the corn dryer below.

Betty Jean uses the base and cover of an old sewing machine but keeps a new machine concealed under the box. A shelf above it holds more pin cushions and make-dos. The make-do on the far left is actually a fabric Christmas ornament that Betty Jean glued to an old bobbin.

Betty Jean made a series of heart shaped pockets using them to display a collection of sewing items.

A carrier holds new and old pin cushions. The strawberry on the far right was hooked by Betty Jean.

Jack added the small platform shelf to the bottom of the grain sifter above which offered Betty Jean an additional creative way to display make-dos. An old Mrs. Butterworth bottle has been converted into a lamp.

Betty Jean purchased the cupboard, bottom left from a shop that was about to close; the shop used to display Yankee Candles.

Betty Jean found the case, which might have been used to dispense candy or gum, at a neighbor's tag sale. She has filled the compartments with buttons, embroidery bobbins, thread and cards of hooks and eyes.

Betty Jean designed and hooked the rug hanging over the three baskets which hold sheep and llama wool.

An old spoon rack becomes the perfect spot to hold a collection of old and new sewing scissors. A folk art doll on the stack of pantry boxes stands out against the wall.

The end of the large work table holds cushions and pantry boxes. Those pieces on the half-round box belonged to Betty Jean's mother who also loved to sew. I asked Betty Jean where she got the 'sewing gene' and she said her mother made all of Betty Jean's clothes out of necessity. She recalls her mother making aprons just as her grandmother did. Betty Jean laughed when she said she learned by making aprons and admitted it seemed as though 'what comes around - goes around'! When Betty Jean was in the sixth grade, she started to make all her own clothes and did so all through high school and college. When she finished college and was on her way to her first job interview, she bought her first store bought dress - a Villager (remember those ladies?) She was so excited to own a store- bought dress that she stored it in a box rather than hang it in the closet.

As a teacher, Betty Jean was drawn initially to samplers with ABC patterns. She has continued her interest in needlework through monthly meetings with a rug hooking group, where she can continue to share and learn. I can understand why she says she hasn't been bored since she retired!

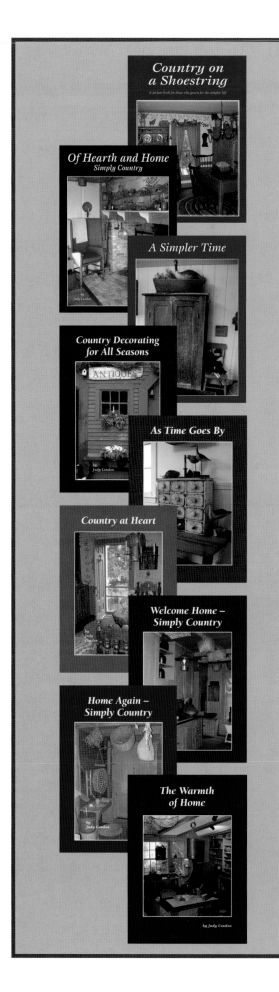

The "simply country" book series

by Judy Condon

Country on a Shoestring
- 33 tips on how to decorate on a shoestring

Of Hearth and Home
- mantels, old painted pieces, signs and primitives

A Simpler Time
- log homes, bedrooms, kitchens, dining rooms, folk art and stencils

Country Decorating for All Seasons
- holiday doors, porches, mantels, trees, vignettes; summer gardens, and fall decorating

As Time Goes By
- The Keeping Room; boxes, baskets and bowls; The Privy; Hallways and Small Ways; The Guest Room

Country at Heart
- The Tavern Room; early looms, dolls and bears; The Gathering Room; a kitchen aged to perfection; country gardens

Welcome Home
- Over 350 photographs from 2 Connecticut homes and 5 Ohio homes.

Home Again
- A house tour book featuring 1 Maine home and 7 Ohio homes including a never before photographed Shaker collection.

The Warmth of Home
- 3 Massachusetts homes, 1 Pennsylvania home, 3 Ohio homes, 1 New York home and 1 Delaware home

The "simply country" book series (cont'd)

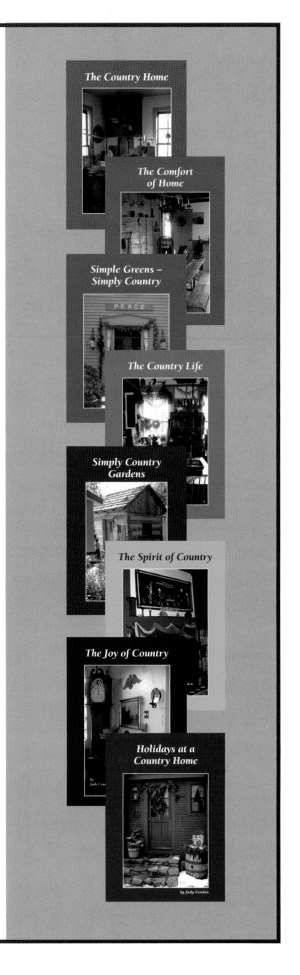

The Country Home
- 6 Ohio homes, 2 Massachusetts homes, and 1 New Hampshire home

The Comfort of Home
- Over 325 color photographs showing a Massachusetts and Ohio home of two exceptional collectors. A Maine home; three Massachusetts homes, one of which is in the city.

Simple Greens – Simply Country
- Over 400 color photographs of country homes decorated for the holidays. Also a chapter on "how to make a country bed" and the recipe for the large decorative gingerbread boys and pantry cakes.

The Country Life
- The home of antique dealer, Marjorie Staufer of Ohio and Colette Donovan of Massachusetts is featured, as well as 4 other Massachusetts homes, a Maine home, a New Hampshire home and a Connecticut home of children's book author, Mark Kimball Moulton.

Simply Country Gardens
- Over 500 color photographs of "just country gardens" from twenty-three homes.

The Spirit of Country
- A house tour format book featuring homes in Virginia, Maine, Connecticut, Indiana, Ohio, Massachusetts, New Hampshire and Kentucky.

The Joy of Country
- Over 400 pictures of homes in Wisconsin, Upstate New York, Ohio, a Connecticut 18thC home, a doublewide in Delaware, 5 Massachusetts homes, a Pennsylvania home and a Maryland home converted from a 19thC granary.

Holidays at a Country Home
- The third holiday book in the series consists of over 500 color photographs of 13 decorated homes and a Condon traditional secret recipe!